UNDERSTANDING GESTALT PLAY THERAPY

FOR BEGINNERS

Empowering Children Through Experiential Learning, Emotional Awareness, Self-Discovery, Creative Expression, And More

DR. ALICIA SONYA

CONTENTS

CHAPTER ONE..................................17

Setting Up A Safe And Nurturing Environment
....17

Creating A Child-Centered Therapy Space ...19

Selecting Materials And Tools For Play 21

Ensuring Emotional And Physical Safety 23

Building Trust And Rapport With Children ..25

Importance Of Privacy And Confidentiality .27

CHAPTER TWO...................................29

Understanding Emotional Awareness In Children..29

Recognizing Emotions In Gestalt Therapy ...31

Helping Children Identify And Express Feelings 33

Techniques To Encourage Emotional Honesty
....35

Overcoming Emotional Blocks And Resistance
....37

Building Emotional Resilience Through Play 39

CHAPTER THREE 41

Techniques For Self-Discovery And Self-Awareness 41

   Guided Imagery And Role-Playing Exercises 43

   Using Puppets, Dolls, And Props For Expression 45

   Encouraging Reflection Through Play Activities 47

   Helping Children Recognize Patterns Of Behavior 49

   Integrating "Here And Now" Experiences ... 51

CHAPTER FOUR 53

Engaging In Creative Expression 53

   Art-Based Techniques For Self-Expression .. 55

   Music, Movement, And Dance In Therapy .. 58

   Storytelling And Narrative Play For Insight . 61

   Symbolic Play And Its Therapeutic Benefits 63

   Balancing Structure With Free Creative Exploration 65

CHAPTER FIVE 69

Essential Gestalt Techniques And Exercises ... 69

Experimenting With The Empty Chair Technique.................71

Role Reversal And Perspective-Taking Exercises.................72

Sensory Awareness Exercises For Grounding 74

Using Gestures And Nonverbal Communication 75

Developing Body Awareness And Mindfulness.................77

CHAPTER SIX.................79

The Role Of The Therapist In Gestalt Play Therapy.................79

Building Empathy And Non-Judgmental Presence.................81

Fostering Collaboration With The Child.......84

Remaining Flexible And Open To Exploration 86

Responding To Verbal And Nonverbal Cues 88

Managing Challenges And Therapeutic Boundaries 91

CHAPTER SEVEN 95

Addressing Common Concerns In Gestalt Play Therapy 95

Overcoming Initial Resistance To Therapy ..97

Dealing With Intense Emotions And Outbursts 99

Managing Parent And Guardian Involvement 101

Adapting Techniques For Different Ages ...103

Handling Sensitive Topics And Trauma......105

CHAPTER EIGHT 107

Detailed FAQs For Beginners......................107

How Does Gestalt Play Therapy Differ From Talk Therapy? 109

What Ages Benefit Most From Gestalt Play Therapy? 111

How Can Parents Support Their Child's Therapy Journey? 114

What Should A First Session Look Like?.....116

What Tools And Resources Can Help In Therapy Sessions? 118

CHAPTER NINE................................121

Tracking Progress And Evaluating Outcomes121

Setting And Reviewing Goals With The Child 123

Methods For Observing Emotional And Behavioral Changes 125

Keeping Session Notes And Reflective Journals 126

Assessing Long-Term Benefits And Growth 128

Adjusting Therapy Approaches Based On Progress 130

Conclusion 132

THE END 136

DISCLAIMER

The information provided in this book is for educational and informational purposes only and is not intended as medical advice, diagnosis, or treatment. Always consult with a qualified healthcare professional before beginning any therapy, practice, or lifestyle change.

The author and publisher of this book make no representations or warranties regarding the accuracy, applicability, or completeness of the content presented. While every effort has been made to ensure the information provided is accurate and up-to-date, the field of health and wellness is constantly evolving, and the reader is advised to use discretion and seek professional guidance as needed.

This book contains references to individuals, products, websites, organizations, or other entities solely for informational purposes. The author and publisher do not endorse, sponsor, or affiliate with any of these references, nor do they receive any benefit from their inclusion. The mention of any names, trademarks, or products does not imply any association or endorsement.

The use of this book is solely at the reader's discretion. Neither the author nor the publisher shall be held liable for any damages, loss, or injury resulting from the use or misuse of the information contained herein.

ABOUT THIS BOOK

Understanding Gestalt Play Therapy For Beginners" serves as a comprehensive resource for therapists, educators, and caregivers, focusing on an engaging and developmentally supportive approach to child therapy. Gestalt Play Therapy combines the unique principles of experiential learning with play, allowing children to explore emotions, discover their identities, and build resilience through dynamic interactions. Unlike traditional forms of therapy that may focus on conversation and cognitive techniques alone, this approach uses play as a bridge to understanding and healing. By integrating concepts like emotional honesty, self-awareness, and creative expression, this book aims to cultivate a robust understanding of the therapy process and its transformative impact on children's mental and emotional growth.

A nurturing, child-centered environment is foundational to effective Gestalt Play Therapy, as it creates a secure space where children can explore their feelings freely. This book emphasizes the importance of setting up a safe and comforting therapy space, selecting appropriate materials and tools, and ensuring both emotional and physical safety. Building trust is essential, and the guide offers valuable insights into fostering a therapeutic relationship where children feel respected and understood. Privacy and confidentiality are also critical, underscoring the therapist's responsibility to protect each child's experiences in the therapeutic setting.

In understanding children's emotions, the book explores how Gestalt Therapy enables children to identify and articulate their feelings—a skill essential for emotional awareness. Through Gestalt techniques, therapists can help children express emotions openly, break through resistance, and build emotional resilience. This approach nurtures a positive environment for exploring feelings, allowing children to gain control over their emotional responses and develop healthier coping mechanisms.

Self-awareness is a core aspect of Gestalt Play Therapy, encouraging children to explore and understand themselves.

This book guides exercises such as role-playing, guided imagery, and using props to assist children in self-reflection. These tools help children recognize patterns in their behavior and connect with the present moment, fostering a deeper understanding of their experiences. This focus on "here and now" experiences allows children to become more self-aware and reflective.

Creative expression is integral to Gestalt Play Therapy, allowing children to communicate complex emotions non-verbally. Through art, music, movement, and symbolic play, children engage in a therapeutic process that goes beyond words, offering them a safe channel for emotional release.

This book emphasizes the value of balancing structure with free exploration, helping therapists create sessions that respect each child's unique expressive style.

To guide the therapeutic journey, the book details essential Gestalt techniques such as the empty chair, sensory awareness exercises, and perspective-taking. These practices encourage children to explore their experiences, both verbally and physically, building body awareness and mindfulness. By using gestures, nonverbal communication, and grounding exercises, children gain a stronger connection to their bodies and emotions, laying the groundwork for growth and self-discovery.

The therapist's role is fundamental to the effectiveness of Gestalt Play Therapy.

A strong emphasis is placed on building empathy, fostering collaboration, and maintaining flexibility within each session. Therapists are encouraged to stay attuned to verbal and nonverbal cues, allowing them to respond to children's needs with sensitivity. This book also addresses handling challenges and maintaining therapeutic boundaries, helping therapists navigate complex situations with professional integrity.

Addressing common concerns in Gestalt Play Therapy, this guide explores strategies for overcoming resistance, managing intense emotions, and involving parents or guardians. It provides practical advice on handling sensitive topics and adapting techniques to suit different age groups, ensuring that the therapy is accessible and impactful for each child's unique needs.

Finally, this book provides practical guidance on tracking progress and evaluating outcomes, helping therapists set meaningful goals and observe emotional and behavioral changes. Reflective journaling, session notes, and goal assessments help therapists monitor each child's development, adjust therapeutic approaches, and ensure that therapy remains effective over time.

The detailed insights and structured framework in this book make it a valuable companion for those dedicated to promoting healing and growth through Gestalt Play Therapy.

CHAPTER ONE

Setting Up A Safe And Nurturing Environment

Creating a safe and nurturing environment is crucial for effective Gestalt play therapy. Begin by choosing a quiet, comfortable space where children can feel relaxed and free from distractions. The room should be well-lit and furnished with soft seating and calming colors. Consider incorporating natural elements, such as plants or soft lighting, to enhance the soothing atmosphere. This physical space allows children to feel secure, fostering an open and honest exploration of their feelings and thoughts.

To further nurture this environment, establish clear boundaries and rules that ensure the child's emotional and physical safety. Explain these rules in simple terms, emphasizing that the therapy space is a judgment-free zone. This helps children understand they can express themselves without fear of negative consequences. Reinforce these boundaries regularly to maintain trust and security throughout the therapeutic process.

Finally, consider the emotional tone you set in the room. Your demeanor should be warm, inviting, and approachable, encouraging children to engage freely. Use positive reinforcement to celebrate their efforts in expressing themselves, which reinforces their sense of safety and trust. When children feel secure, they are more likely to explore their emotions and experiences, leading to a more productive therapy session.

Creating A Child-Centered Therapy Space

A child-centered therapy space prioritizes the needs and preferences of the child, allowing them to lead their healing process. Begin by involving the child in designing the therapy space. Ask for their input on colors, themes, and favorite items they would like to include. This can empower them and help establish a sense of ownership, making them feel more comfortable and willing to engage in the therapeutic process.

In addition to aesthetics, consider the layout of the space. Arrange furniture and materials to create distinct areas for different types of play, such as art, storytelling, and movement. This variety allows children to choose how they want to express themselves and interact with their feelings. Keep the area uncluttered and organized, which can help minimize distractions and facilitate smoother transitions between activities.

Finally, incorporate elements that reflect the child's interests and experiences, such as toys, books, or art supplies relevant to their life. These familiar items can spark connection and engagement, encouraging the child to open up and share their thoughts. A well-designed child-centered space is not only inviting but also tailored to support the individual needs of each child, making it an essential aspect of Gestalt play therapy.

Selecting Materials And Tools For Play

Choosing the right materials and tools for play is essential to facilitate meaningful expression in Gestalt therapy. Start by gathering a variety of art supplies, such as crayons, markers, paints, and clay, which can help children express emotions they may not have the words for. Additionally, includes puppets, dolls, and action figures, allowing children to act out scenarios and explore their feelings in a non-threatening way.

Incorporate sensory materials like sand, water, or fabric to engage children's tactile senses. These materials can be soothing and grounding, enabling children to relax and open up during sessions.

For example, using sand trays can provide a safe space for children to create and manipulate their environment, which often reflects their internal world. Be mindful of any potential allergies or sensitivities when selecting materials to ensure a comfortable experience.

Finally, consider the developmental stage of the child when selecting materials. Younger children may benefit from more tactile and simple items, while older children might prefer more complex tools like storytelling kits or role-play scenarios. Regularly refresh the materials to maintain the child's interest and invite new forms of expression. Thoughtfully selected materials can significantly enhance the therapeutic experience and foster deeper emotional exploration.

Ensuring Emotional And Physical Safety

Emotional and physical safety are fundamental components of effective Gestalt play therapy.

Begin by establishing clear guidelines regarding physical interactions and boundaries during play. Explain to children that they have the right to say no to any activity that makes them uncomfortable. This empowers them to take control of their experience, ensuring they feel secure throughout the therapeutic process.

To foster emotional safety, create a supportive atmosphere that encourages open dialogue about feelings and experiences. Actively listen to children, validating their emotions and providing a space for them to express themselves without fear of judgment.

Use gentle prompts and questions to guide conversations, allowing children to explore their feelings in a safe environment. Reinforcing the idea that all emotions are acceptable can help children understand their experiences better and feel validated in their expressions.

Regularly assess the safety of the environment throughout sessions. Be observant of signs of distress or discomfort in the child, and be prepared to adjust the activities or materials accordingly. Creating a feedback loop where children feel comfortable sharing their feelings about the space and activities will enhance their sense of safety.

A focus on emotional and physical safety encourages children to engage more fully in the therapeutic process, allowing for deeper healing.

Building Trust And Rapport With Children

Building trust and rapport is essential for effective therapy with children. Start by showing genuine interest in the child's thoughts and feelings. Engage in active listening, making eye contact, and reflecting on what they share to show understanding. Use open body language and a warm tone to convey that you are approachable and supportive, creating a welcoming atmosphere where children feel comfortable sharing their feelings. Consistency in sessions helps establish trust. Arrive on time, follow through on promises, and maintain a routine that allows children to know what to expect. This predictability provides a sense of security, helping children feel more at ease during sessions. Over time, they will come to rely on you as a safe person in their lives, fostering a deeper therapeutic relationship.

Incorporate play and humor into the therapeutic process to enhance rapport. Engaging in shared activities that the child enjoys can strengthen your connection and create a more relaxed environment. Allowing children to take the lead during play can also empower them, reinforcing their autonomy and encouraging openness. Building trust and rapport takes time, but it is a vital foundation for successful Gestalt play therapy.

Importance Of Privacy And Confidentiality

Privacy and confidentiality are cornerstones of a trusting therapeutic relationship. At the beginning of therapy, explain the importance of keeping what is discussed in sessions private. Clarify any exceptions to confidentiality, such as situations involving safety concerns.

This transparency helps children understand that they can share their thoughts and feelings without fear of their personal information being disclosed to others.

To reinforce confidentiality, consider using a "therapeutic agreement" that outlines the boundaries of privacy. This can be a simple document or a verbal agreement made with the child (and their caregivers) at the outset. Regularly revisiting this agreement throughout therapy can help maintain awareness and comfort around confidentiality, allowing children to feel secure in their expressions.

Additionally, create a space where children can engage in therapy without interruptions or eavesdropping. This includes using soundproofing techniques or scheduling sessions at times when the therapy space is least likely to be accessed by others. By prioritizing privacy, you demonstrate respect for the child's personal experiences, fostering a safe environment that encourages open communication and exploration.

CHAPTER TWO

Understanding Emotional Awareness In Children

Emotional awareness in children forms the foundation of effective Gestalt play therapy. The process involves guiding children to notice and understand their emotions, which often manifest through behaviors, body language, and non-verbal cues. In therapy sessions, therapists use play as a bridge to help children connect with their feelings, whether it's through storytelling, drawing, or role-playing. This method fosters a safe environment for the child to recognize the sensations tied to emotions, such as excitement, sadness, or frustration.

To make emotional awareness relatable, therapists introduce basic language around feelings. Using emotion cards or visual aids, children learn to identify different emotional states.

A common exercise might involve asking the child to select a card that represents how they feel at the moment, encouraging them to articulate why they chose it. This process helps children build a vocabulary for their feelings and cultivates a deeper understanding of their internal experiences.

By acknowledging their emotions, children gradually develop self-awareness and a sense of control over their reactions. This awareness empowers them to make choices about how to handle emotions instead of being overwhelmed by them.

Over time, consistent practice during sessions enables children to become more attuned to their emotional responses and learn how to manage them in everyday situations, thus setting a solid foundation for emotional health.

Recognizing Emotions In Gestalt Therapy

Recognizing emotions is central to Gestalt play therapy, where therapists work with children to observe and validate what they feel without judgment. This process involves guiding the child to focus on their immediate experience and labeling it accurately. For example, a child might be asked, "How does your body feel when you're mad?" This encourages a child to identify bodily sensations connected to their emotions, promoting mindfulness and fostering a stronger connection to their emotional states.

Therapists might use tools such as dolls or puppets to enact scenarios that reflect the child's experiences. By doing so, children can safely express emotions they may not fully understand or feel comfortable addressing directly. For instance, if a child is angry, they might have a puppet express this anger toward another toy, allowing the child to observe and discuss it from a safer, distanced perspective.

As the child learns to recognize different emotions, they gain confidence in naming and discussing them. This approach demystifies emotions, making them feel less overwhelming and more manageable. Through repetition and supportive interactions, children become adept at identifying what they feel, which in turn fosters emotional intelligence and sets the groundwork for healthier self-expression?

Helping Children Identify And Express Feelings

Helping children identify and express their feelings is a key goal in Gestalt play therapy, achieved by creating activities that bring emotions to the surface in a playful yet insightful manner. One approach is to use art therapy techniques, like drawing or painting, where children depict their emotions through colors or shapes.

The therapist might ask questions about the artwork to encourage the child to reflect on and verbalize their emotional experience.

Another method includes storytelling, where children invent characters experiencing similar emotions to their own. As the story unfolds, they can project their feelings onto these characters, helping them articulate what they may find difficult to express about themselves. By allowing the child to observe from a safe distance, storytelling encourages emotional openness and helps them connect with their inner thoughts.

This process of identifying and expressing emotions allows children to experience a sense of relief and clarity. They realize that their feelings are valid and manageable, which builds confidence in handling difficult emotions. Through these expressive techniques, children also learn that emotions can be discussed and shared, creating a foundation for honest and open emotional communication as they grow.

Techniques To Encourage Emotional Honesty

Encouraging emotional honesty is vital in Gestalt play therapy, where therapists guide children toward openly recognizing and expressing their true feelings. Role-playing games serve as a valuable tool here; children might act out situations using toys or costumes, enabling them to express emotions that may be suppressed or hidden in real life. This safe and playful setting allows them to explore honest reactions without fear of judgment.

Active listening is another crucial technique. Therapists model empathy and validation, repeating back the child's words or mirroring their emotions to show understanding. For example, if a child expresses fear, the therapist might say, "It sounds like you're feeling really scared about that." This validation builds trust, showing the child that it's safe to be truthful about their emotions, and fostering authenticity in their self-expression.

Therapists also use a technique called "I statements," encouraging children to phrase feelings as "I feel" rather than placing blame or making external statements. This practice teaches children to take ownership of their emotions, promoting emotional responsibility. Over time, children learn to articulate their feelings directly and transparently, leading to healthier communication habits both within and outside of therapy.

Overcoming Emotional Blocks And Resistance

In Gestalt play therapy, overcoming emotional blocks and resistance is a common focus, as children often struggle to confront uncomfortable emotions. One effective method is to introduce gradual exposure, where therapists slowly bring up challenging topics, such as fear or anger, in a way that feels manageable for the child. For example, a therapist might discuss a scenario indirectly or through play, helping the child address difficult feelings without immediate intensity.

Using creative tools, such as sand trays or clay modeling, allows children to externalize blocked emotions in a non-verbal way, giving shape and form to their internal experiences. By creating scenes that symbolize their feelings, children become more comfortable exploring what they might otherwise resist. This tactile approach allows them to confront their emotions safely, breaking down barriers gradually.

Therapists may also gently confront resistance by acknowledging it with the child, making statements like, "It seems like it's hard to talk about this," which validates their experience and reduces the power of resistance. This approach helps children feel seen and understood, encouraging them to trust the process. Gradually, they develop greater openness and previously avoided feelings become more approachable.

Building Emotional Resilience Through Play

Building emotional resilience through play is a cornerstone of Gestalt therapy, as it allows children to develop coping skills for future emotional challenges. The play offers an engaging way for children to practice bouncing back from disappointment or frustration in a controlled environment. Activities like board games or cooperative tasks require patience and adaptability, helping children experience minor setbacks in a low-stakes setting.

Role-playing also contributes significantly to resilience, as it allows children to act out potential real-life scenarios. For instance, they might enact an argument between friends and practice resolving it calmly. Through guided discussion, therapists help children explore healthier responses to these challenges, fostering confidence and adaptive thinking.

Over time, these playful encounters build a stronger emotional foundation. Children learn that they can face difficulties and find solutions, empowering them to handle more significant obstacles as they grow. As they become accustomed to navigating emotions through play, they carry these skills beyond therapy, equipped with resilience that supports them in real-life situations.

CHAPTER THREE

Techniques For Self-Discovery And Self-Awareness

In Gestalt play therapy, self-discovery is fostered by creating a safe and supportive environment for the child to explore their emotions, thoughts, and behaviors. Practitioners guide children in recognizing and expressing their feelings without judgment, allowing them to start identifying personal strengths and challenges. Through activities like drawing and storytelling, therapists encourage children to connect with their inner experiences, helping them become more aware of themselves.

A practical technique involves setting up scenarios where children can explore specific feelings or situations they have encountered. For instance, a therapist might ask a child to draw a "feelings map" of where different emotions are felt in their body, helping them gain insight into how emotions affect their physical experience. Through this exercise, children start to notice their emotions' impact and can learn to process them with a greater sense of control.

Therapists also use gentle guidance to help children articulate their discoveries in words, further reinforcing self-awareness. By regularly reflecting on these experiences, children gain an evolving understanding of themselves, and with this knowledge, they can better handle challenging situations and make more informed choices.

Self-discovery becomes a transformative process, empowering the child to navigate their world with greater clarity and resilience.

Guided Imagery And Role-Playing Exercises

Guided imagery in Gestalt play therapy helps children visualize scenarios that allow for deeper self-exploration and emotional release. The therapist guides the child through a series of images, prompting them to imagine a place or situation where they feel safe, happy, or empowered.

For example, the therapist might ask, "Imagine you're in a magical forest. What do you see around you? How do you feel?" This practice helps children access emotions they may struggle to express verbally.

Role-playing exercises go hand-in-hand with guided imagery, allowing children to act out roles that represent their inner conflicts, desires, or relationships. For instance, a child might role-play as a "superhero" to confront fear, giving them a sense of strength and confidence to approach real-life challenges.

The therapist may also take on a role, allowing the child to "talk to" their fears or other characters representing significant people or emotions in their life.

In both guided imagery and role-playing, children gain a safe outlet to express thoughts and feelings indirectly. This approach allows them to process emotions without feeling overwhelmed, as they are stepping into a role or a world that feels separate from their everyday self. As they do, children build coping skills, learn to handle anxiety and develop a positive approach to confronting difficult emotions.

Using Puppets, Dolls, And Props For Expression

Puppets, dolls, and props are powerful tools in Gestalt play therapy for helping children express emotions and scenarios that may be difficult to verbalize. When a child uses a puppet or doll, it becomes a stand-in for their thoughts or experiences, enabling them to project feelings onto the character.

This makes it easier for the child to explore complex emotions, often revealing thoughts and fears they haven't yet verbalized.

In practice, a therapist might introduce a doll and ask, "How does this doll feel today?" allowing the child to create a story that indirectly reveals their emotional state. Children often feel safer sharing feelings when they feel like they are speaking through the puppet or doll, removing the pressure of direct self-disclosure. This role-playing helps them gain insight into their emotions, as they externalize and "talk" through the character they control.

Props are also used to set up specific scenarios, such as a family dinner or a playground scene, allowing the child to navigate social situations in a controlled environment. This helps them express responses to real-life settings, reinforcing the understanding of cause and effect in social interactions. Through this process, children become more comfortable recognizing, sharing, and processing emotions.

Encouraging Reflection Through Play Activities

Reflection is essential in Gestalt play therapy as it helps children process their experiences and develop self-awareness. Play activities like art, sand trays, or storytelling encourage children to revisit and reflect on their actions, emotions, and decisions. By guiding a child to recreate a troubling scenario in the sand tray, for example, therapists help the child process feelings and consider alternate ways to cope.

Reflection often involves discussing the child's choices within the play session.

For instance, after a child creates a scene, the therapist might ask, "What made you choose that character?" or "How does this story end?" Such open-ended questions encourage children to think about their actions and feelings, helping them to make connections and recognize patterns in their behavior. This gentle reflection allows them to build emotional resilience and understand the impact of their reactions.

Through repeated reflection, children learn to identify emotions, assess situations, and practice self-regulation. They gain insights into how their feelings influence their behavior and decision-making, which is crucial for developing coping strategies and emotional awareness.

This process is integral to helping children apply what they learn in therapy to real-life situations.

Helping Children Recognize Patterns Of Behavior

Gestalt play therapy helps children recognize behavior patterns by using activities that reflect their choices and actions. For example, the therapist might notice if a child consistently plays the role of the "victim" in pretend scenarios, suggesting an underlying pattern of feeling powerless.

By pointing out these patterns gently, the therapist helps the child become more conscious of how they approach situations and relationships.

One practical approach is for the therapist to introduce themes and see if the child's behavior changes. If the child always reacts with anger or sadness in a specific role, this pattern can be explored further. The therapist might say, "I noticed you feel sad when playing this role. Let's explore why." This reflection allows the child to consider if they often feel this way in similar real-life situations, helping them recognize recurring feelings and behaviors.

As children become more aware of these patterns, they gain the ability to make different choices. They learn that just as they can change roles in play, they can approach real-life situations differently. By identifying and understanding behavior patterns, children are empowered to create new responses that are healthier and more adaptive in real-life scenarios.

Integrating "Here And Now" Experiences

The "here and now" principle in Gestalt play therapy emphasizes the importance of being present in the moment. Therapists encourage children to focus on their current feelings and experiences rather than past or future concerns. By saying, "What are you feeling right now?" therapists help children connect with their present emotions, promoting awareness of how they feel in real time.

In practice, therapists use grounding techniques to keep children engaged in the present. For instance, a therapist might ask a child to describe a toy's texture, color, or shape, keeping their focus on immediate sensations. By doing so, children learn to understand how their physical sensations connect to their emotions, building a stronger sense of self-awareness and helping them become more attuned to their emotional responses.

This "here and now" focus fosters mindfulness, teaching children to process emotions as they arise rather than avoiding or suppressing them. Over time, children learn to recognize and address their feelings without feeling overwhelmed. This awareness equips them with the skills to manage emotions proactively, helping them build resilience and confidence in facing life's challenges.

CHAPTER FOUR

Engaging In Creative Expression

In Gestalt play therapy, engaging in creative expression allows children to tap into their emotions and communicate in ways beyond words. This method encourages kids to use tools like drawing, sculpting, or creating collages as a way of projecting their inner world. For instance, a child may create a clay figure that represents a challenging situation they're experiencing, helping them to externalize and process complex emotions. By providing different mediums, therapists give children the freedom to choose the form that resonates with them most, fostering a sense of agency and self-discovery.

Creative expression is a two-way process in Gestalt therapy, with therapists actively participating alongside children to create a safe, playful environment.

This can mean sitting on the floor with the child, engaging in art-making, or mirroring their actions with encouragement. Therapists might comment on specific aspects of the child's work, such as, "I notice you chose a lot of bright colors here—can you tell me more about that?" Such reflections allow the child to recognize and verbalize their feelings, making the therapy session feel more like a shared experience than a traditional "session."

Finally, creative expression in Gestalt therapy focuses on enhancing self-awareness and connection to the present moment.

Activities often begin with grounding exercises, like taking deep breaths or stretching, to help children center themselves. This focus on the here-and-now allows the child to immerse themselves in the creative task without judgment. Therapists encourage children to describe how they feel during the activity, which builds mindfulness and a clearer self-concept. Over time, this process of creative expression helps children understand and manage their emotions constructively.

Art-Based Techniques For Self-Expression

Art-based techniques in Gestalt play therapy serve as an accessible avenue for children to express feelings they may not fully understand or know how to verbalize. Techniques such as drawing, painting, and crafting enable children to explore and project their emotions in a way that feels safe and supported. For example, therapists might invite a child to "draw what a difficult day looks like" or "create a mask that represents how you feel." This use of symbolism encourages children to convey inner experiences indirectly, making it easier for them to address sensitive or complex emotions.

During sessions, therapists may guide children in interpreting their artwork, which aids in developing self-awareness.

Rather than analyzing the child's art themselves, therapists use open-ended questions like, "What stands out to you in this picture?" or "How does this part of the painting make you feel?" By doing so, children can connect their artwork to real-life situations, deepening their understanding of their emotional state. This active, curious approach also fosters a therapeutic alliance, where children feel respected and understood rather than judged or evaluated.

Art-based therapy techniques are highly adaptable, allowing therapists to tailor activities to each child's needs and developmental level. For younger children, simple exercises such as coloring shapes that represent different emotions can be effective. Older children, on the other hand, might be encouraged to work on more intricate projects, like creating a "storyboard" of events that affected them.

These activities are a practical way to promote self-exploration and emotional expression, helping children gradually build resilience and self-confidence.

Music, Movement, And Dance In Therapy

In Gestalt play therapy, music, movement, and dance offer powerful ways for children to express themselves, especially for those who struggle with verbal communication. Dance and movement exercises encourage children to use their bodies as a means of exploring and expressing emotions.

For instance, a therapist might play a specific song and ask the child to move in a way that reflects how the music makes them feel, helping to externalize feelings like happiness, anger, or sadness. This approach leverages the body's natural ability to process emotions physically, making it particularly effective for children who have experienced trauma.

Music in therapy sessions can serve as both a comforting and expressive outlet. Children might be invited to play simple musical instruments, experiment with different sounds, or even create their songs. This process of musical improvisation is beneficial in developing self-expression and confidence. Additionally, certain types of music can help regulate emotions, acting as a grounding tool when children are feeling overwhelmed. Therapists can also encourage children to explore rhythm, which helps them connect more deeply with their emotions and the present moment.

Dance and movement activities also encourage a deeper mind-body connection, which is essential in Gestalt therapy. Simple exercises, like mirroring movements with the therapist, can help children feel seen and understood, while free-form dance allows them to experience a sense of freedom and release.

Therapists might encourage children to visualize emotions as they move, helping them "dance out" stress or frustration. This dynamic form of play therapy provides children with an engaging, non-verbal way to navigate complex emotions and bodily experiences, promoting healing and self-discovery.

Storytelling And Narrative Play For Insight

Storytelling and narrative play in Gestalt therapy provides children with a unique way to explore personal experiences and make sense of their emotions. By creating fictional stories, children can project their feelings and experiences onto characters, making it easier to explore challenging situations.

A therapist might invite a child to "tell a story about a brave hero" or "imagine a world where they feel safe and strong." This distance allows children to confront difficult emotions without feeling overwhelmed, offering a safer way to process their own stories.

The role of the therapist is to guide and support the storytelling process, encouraging children to explore different aspects of their narratives. This might involve asking questions about the character's feelings or actions, such as, "Why do you think the hero felt that way?" or "What would they do next?" This form of questioning allows children to delve into their feelings indirectly, facilitating greater self-awareness. Through narrative play, therapists can help children identify recurring themes in their stories, which may mirror real-life concerns, fears, or desires.

Storytelling as a therapeutic tool also promotes problem-solving and resilience. For instance, a therapist might suggest a plot twist where the character overcomes a challenge, allowing the child to brainstorm ways to cope with difficulties in their own lives.

By "rewriting" parts of the story, children learn that they, too, can influence the outcomes of their experiences. This helps build a sense of empowerment and hope, as children realize they can create positive change in their lives.

Symbolic Play And Its Therapeutic Benefits

Symbolic play, a cornerstone of Gestalt play therapy, enables children to use objects, toys, and actions to represent real-life experiences, facilitating emotional expression. Through role-playing, children might act out scenarios with dolls, action figures, or puppets that mirror real-life situations they're navigating.

For instance, a child might use a toy to represent a family member and "talk" to it, expressing feelings they may otherwise find hard to share. This form of indirect communication allows children to project complex emotions, making the therapeutic process safer and less intimidating.

Therapists play an active role in supporting symbolic play, observing and reflecting on the child's actions without interfering.

If a child enacts a scene of conflict or anxiety, the therapist might comment empathetically, saying, "It seems like this doll feels left out—does that happen sometimes?" Such gentle prompts encourage children to explore their feelings without pressure. Therapists may also introduce new toys or props to gently guide the child in exploring different aspects of their world, like bringing in animal figurines to symbolize specific feelings or personalities.

Symbolic play offers children a sense of control and mastery over their experiences. They can rewrite scenarios or change outcomes in ways they may not be able to in real life, which is empowering and therapeutic.

For example, a child who feels powerless in a certain situation might find confidence by role-playing as a character who successfully overcomes a challenge. Over time, this therapeutic process helps children work through internal conflicts, manage stress, and build coping skills in a playful yet meaningful way.

Balancing Structure With Free Creative Exploration

In Gestalt play therapy, balancing structure with free creative exploration is essential to meet the diverse needs of each child. The structure provides a predictable, safe environment while allowing room for spontaneity and encourages genuine self-expression.

A session may start with a structured activity, like drawing or storytelling, which serves as a familiar anchor. Once the child feels comfortable, the therapist may encourage them to lead the direction of the activity, perhaps by choosing their art supplies or deciding how they'd like to expand the story.

This balance between guidance and freedom fosters trust and creativity. Therapists use structured activities strategically to create a therapeutic rhythm, helping children ease into more open-ended exploration.

For instance, a session may begin with a grounding exercise like deep breathing, followed by a structured task, and then gradually transition into free play. In doing so, the child feels both supported and empowered to explore their feelings. The therapist might say, "Let's see what happens next," allowing the child to take ownership of the session's direction. This balance builds a sense of security and flexibility in the therapeutic relationship.

Free creative exploration, though less structured, is equally valuable in helping children experience a sense of agency and personal expression.

During these moments, children may experiment with different materials or activities without any specific instructions, guided by their interests and intuition. This process encourages children to listen to their inner voice and explore their unique way of self-expression, fostering self-trust and emotional resilience. Through this balanced approach, children learn to navigate boundaries, self-regulate and embrace both structure and spontaneity in a way that supports emotional growth.

CHAPTER FIVE

Essential Gestalt Techniques And Exercises

Gestalt therapy emphasizes self-awareness, personal responsibility, and being present in the moment. Essential techniques used in Gestalt play therapy help children express their emotions creatively and safely. One key principle is staying in the "here and now," encouraging children to explore what they feel in the present rather than focusing on past events. The therapist acts as a guide, facilitating activities that help the child process unresolved feelings through action rather than just conversation.

For example, in sessions, therapists may ask children to draw what they are feeling, make figures with clay, or reenact emotional events through play. These activities allow emotions to surface naturally, bypassing cognitive barriers. The therapist continuously observes for patterns, such as avoidance behaviors, and uses them as opportunities to prompt reflection and discussion.

A playful and relaxed environment is essential for children to engage comfortably. Techniques like puppetry or sand play also allow children to project their thoughts onto external objects, creating a safe emotional distance. By immersing the child in active experiences, Gestalt therapy ensures their emotions are processed holistically—emotionally, physically, and mentally.

Experimenting With The Empty Chair Technique

The empty chair technique is widely used in Gestalt play therapy to help children externalize emotions and communicate with parts of themselves or others. The therapist places an empty chair in front of the child, encouraging them to imagine that a person or an emotion, like fear or anger, is sitting in the chair. The child can then talk to the chair as if speaking to someone directly.

In practice, if a child feels angry at a parent, they can pretend the parent is in the chair and express their frustrations freely. The therapist encourages honesty and emotional release, guiding the child to explore what they would say or how they feel without interruptions or fear of judgment. This creates space for unexpressed emotions to surface.

The process may also involve switching roles. After the child expresses their side, the therapist might ask the child to sit in the empty chair and respond as if they were the other person or feeling. This helps the child gain perspective, develop empathy, and discover new ways of understanding difficult emotions.

Role Reversal And Perspective-Taking Exercises

Role reversal allows children to step into the shoes of another person, animal, or even an imaginary object to develop empathy and insight. The child might play the role of a teacher, parent, or even a superhero, while the therapist plays the child. This role-playing activity gives children a chance to understand others' viewpoints and feelings more clearly.

For example, a child upset with their sibling might act as the sibling while the therapist takes the child's role. During the process, the child gains insight into how their actions might affect others, fostering self-awareness. The therapist can gently guide the role play by asking questions like, "How does it feel to be your sibling right now?" or "What do you think your sibling needs from you?"

These exercises also empower children to experiment with different responses to conflicts. Through repeated role-playing scenarios, they learn healthy ways to navigate emotions like frustration, sadness, or jealousy.

It fosters emotional flexibility, helping children see beyond their immediate perspectives and practice emotional regulation.

Sensory Awareness Exercises For Grounding

Sensory awareness exercises are designed to ground children in the present moment by focusing on their five senses—sight, sound, smell, taste, and touch. The goal is to reduce anxiety and help children regulate overwhelming emotions by connecting with their bodies and environment.

A typical exercise might involve the "5-4-3-2-1 technique," where the child is asked to identify five things they see, four they feel, three they hear, two they smell, and one they taste. This structured focus on sensory input helps shift attention away from distressing thoughts and brings them back to the present.

Therapists may also use sensory tools like textured objects, scented playdough, or calming sounds to engage the child. These activities not only enhance emotional regulation but also build awareness of how different sensory inputs affect mood. Over time, children can use these exercises independently as a coping strategy during stressful situations.

Using Gestures And Nonverbal Communication

Gestalt therapy emphasizes the importance of nonverbal communication, especially with children who may struggle to articulate their feelings verbally.

Therapists pay close attention to gestures, facial expressions, and body language as they often reveal emotions that words cannot.

In a session, the therapist might ask a child to show how they feel through a gesture—like stomping their feet to represent anger or curling into a ball to show sadness. These nonverbal actions help children express their emotions physically, especially when they lack the vocabulary to explain them.

Sometimes, the therapist mirrors the child's body language to validate their experience and build rapport. This creates a sense of safety and trust, making the child feel understood. Through consistent practice, children learn to recognize the connection between their emotions and physical reactions, improving their emotional awareness.

Developing Body Awareness And Mindfulness

Body awareness exercises in Gestalt therapy help children notice and understand physical sensations associated with emotions. The goal is to teach children how their bodies react to stress, fear, or joy and how to respond in healthier ways.

A practical example is a "body scan" exercise, where the therapist guides the child to focus on different parts of their body, noticing sensations without judgment. This might start with, "What do your feet feel like right now?" and gradually move up to other body parts.

The therapist may ask follow-up questions, such as, "Where do you feel nervousness in your body?"

Over time, these mindfulness practices help children develop an early warning system for stress. They become aware of physical tension or discomfort before emotions escalate, giving them the chance to use calming strategies. Through such exercises, children build a deeper connection with their bodies, learning to regulate emotions in healthier ways.

CHAPTER SIX

The Role Of The Therapist In Gestalt Play Therapy

In Gestalt play therapy, the therapist plays a dynamic role, focusing on establishing a safe environment where the child feels understood and supported. This involves being fully present in each session, actively observing, and responding to the child's behavior, emotions, and interactions with their surroundings. The therapist does not impose interpretations but instead facilitates the child's self-discovery through carefully guided interactions. By creating an atmosphere of acceptance, the therapist encourages the child to explore their thoughts and feelings openly, helping them to develop self-awareness and emotional resilience.

The therapist's role extends to actively engaging the child in play activities that resonate with their unique experiences. This may involve using toys, art, storytelling, and role-playing, allowing the child to express complex emotions and unresolved issues in a non-threatening way. Through these creative methods, the therapist gently guides the child towards self-discovery, allowing them to work through past experiences, fears, or conflicts. The therapist's presence is consistent but not intrusive, acting as a compassionate witness to the child's unfolding narrative.

Additionally, the therapist adapts their approach to the child's developmental level, needs, and preferences. This adaptability is essential in Gestalt play therapy as it ensures that therapeutic techniques remain relevant and accessible to the child. By remaining attuned to the child's pace and responses, the therapist facilitates a healing process that feels natural and supportive, allowing the child to gain confidence in exploring and processing their inner experiences.

Building Empathy And Non-Judgmental Presence

Empathy and non-judgmental presence form the foundation of trust in Gestalt play therapy, creating a space where the child feels truly seen and valued. The therapist models empathy by listening attentively and reflecting on the child's feelings and experiences, which helps the child feel understood. Rather than offering judgments or solutions, the therapist gently acknowledges the child's emotional state, showing acceptance and respect for their personal experiences. This unconditional positive regard encourages the child to express themselves openly without fear of judgment.

Through empathic listening and responses, the therapist fosters an environment of acceptance, where the child can explore their emotions safely.

For example, if a child expresses frustration through play, the therapist might say, "It looks like that character is feeling frustrated—can you show me more about what's happening?" This approach allows the child to project their feelings onto the play, making it easier to identify and work through their emotions. The therapist's validation of these emotions helps the child feel that their experiences are real and important, fostering self-acceptance.

Maintaining a non-judgmental presence also means that the therapist stays mindful of their reactions and assumptions, ensuring that they remain open and fully present for the child. This requires a conscious effort to set aside biases and focus solely on the child's perspective. By being a calm, neutral, and supportive presence, the therapist builds a sense of safety that encourages the child to take emotional risks, explore challenging topics, and ultimately develop greater self-awareness.

Fostering Collaboration With The Child

Fostering collaboration in Gestalt play therapy involves inviting the child to actively participate in their healing journey. The therapist treats the child as a co-creator in the therapeutic process, allowing them to take the lead in deciding what they want to explore during sessions. This approach empowers the child, making them feel valued and in control of their healing journey. Collaboration might involve asking the child which toys or activities they want to use or encouraging them to share ideas about how a story might unfold.

The therapist reinforces this collaborative relationship by frequently checking in with the child, showing interest in their ideas, and respecting their choices.

For example, if the child decides to create a story using toys, the therapist might ask questions like, "What should happen next?" or "How does this character feel?" This encourages the child to think critically and explore their thoughts and emotions creatively and constructively. The therapist's role is supportive rather than directive, allowing the child to experiment and express their thoughts at their own pace.

Moreover, the therapist uses collaborative techniques to strengthen the therapeutic alliance, making the child feel more comfortable and willing to engage. By aligning with the child's interests, the therapist creates a bond that motivates the child to actively participate and feel more invested in their progress. The collaborative nature of Gestalt play therapy helps the child develop decision-making skills, self-confidence, and the ability to articulate their emotions, fostering a greater sense of personal agency and resilience.

Remaining Flexible And Open To Exploration

Flexibility is essential in Gestalt play therapy as it allows the therapist to adapt to the child's needs, emotions, and shifting energy levels throughout the session. Each child and each session can bring new dynamics, so the therapist remains open to unexpected changes in direction. If a child starts with one activity but loses interest, the therapist may suggest another approach or follow the child's lead, allowing them to explore different avenues of expression. This flexibility helps keep the child engaged and shows them that their interests and feelings are valued.

By maintaining openness, the therapist encourages spontaneous expression, creating opportunities for the child to explore feelings they may not have anticipated discussing. For instance, a child might start with building blocks but shift to drawing or storytelling when a particular emotion arises. The therapist adjusts to these changes, making room for the child to explore deeper feelings as they come up naturally.

This flexibility builds trust and allows the child to feel more comfortable expressing a range of emotions and experiences without feeling restricted.

Remaining open to exploration also means embracing the child's unique ways of processing emotions and ideas. The therapist refrains from having a fixed agenda and instead supports the child's journey of discovery. This approach reinforces that healing is a fluid and organic process, empowering the child to take ownership of their growth and self-discovery in a safe, adaptable space.

Responding To Verbal And Nonverbal Cues

Responding to both verbal and nonverbal cues is crucial in Gestalt play therapy, as children often communicate their thoughts and emotions through body language, play, and facial expressions. The therapist observes the child's behavior closely, noting subtle shifts in tone, body posture, or eye contact that may indicate how they feel. For example, a child may avoid eye contact when discussing a difficult topic, signaling discomfort or fear. The therapist acknowledges these cues gently, perhaps by mirroring the child's expression or inviting them to share more about their feelings.

In recognizing nonverbal cues, the therapist helps the child understand and label their emotions, fostering self-awareness and emotional intelligence. For instance, if a child looks tense while playing, the therapist might say, "I see that your hands are holding that toy tightly—what's happening in the story right now?" This allows the child to connect their physical reactions with emotional experiences, enhancing their understanding of how feelings manifest. By validating these cues, the therapist encourages the child to become more attuned to their inner experiences.

Moreover, when the child does express themselves verbally, the therapist listens attentively, responding in a way that reflects understanding without interrupting or redirecting. This reinforces the child's sense of agency and supports their journey toward self-discovery.

By skillfully responding to both verbal and nonverbal signals, the therapist creates a responsive environment where the child feels heard and understood on multiple levels.

Managing Challenges And Therapeutic Boundaries

In Gestalt play therapy, managing challenges and maintaining therapeutic boundaries are essential to ensure a safe and productive space for the child. Children may sometimes exhibit challenging behaviors, such as resistance, withdrawal, or defiance, especially when facing difficult emotions. The therapist handles these behaviors with patience and empathy, recognizing that they are often expressions of underlying issues. Rather than reacting with frustration, the therapist might use reflective techniques or gentle prompts to help the child feel supported and understood, allowing them to gradually open up.

Setting clear boundaries is also crucial, as it helps the child feel safe and understand the limits within the therapeutic relationship. For example, the therapist might explain that certain behaviors, like throwing toys or aggressive actions, are not permitted while offering alternative ways to express strong emotions. By maintaining consistent boundaries, the therapist creates a secure environment where the child feels respected and learns to respect others. These boundaries provide structure while still allowing room for exploration, helping the child build trust in the therapeutic relationship.

Additionally, the therapist models healthy ways of handling challenges by remaining calm and supportive, teaching the child constructive responses to difficulties. This approach reinforces that challenges are part of the healing process and can be approached with openness and resilience. By managing challenges with empathy and maintaining clear boundaries, the therapist provides a stable, respectful environment where the child can explore their feelings and behaviors safely, promoting emotional growth and self-awareness.

CHAPTER SEVEN

Addressing Common Concerns In Gestalt Play Therapy

In Gestalt Play Therapy, children often express concerns through play, which serves as their natural language. A common initial concern is unfamiliarity with the therapeutic process. To address this, the therapist creates a welcoming space filled with various play materials—such as puppets, clay, or drawings—that allow children to feel comfortable and safe. By inviting the child to explore these items without pressure, the therapist builds rapport and establishes trust.

Some children may also feel hesitant or unsure about expressing their feelings directly. The therapist can address this by modeling emotional expression through playful characters or engaging in collaborative storytelling. This technique helps the child see how to express emotions constructively, making it easier to engage with deeper topics. When children observe their therapist approaching feelings openly and playfully, it reduces their discomfort with emotional expression.

Additionally, children may struggle to understand the purpose of therapy. Therapists can use metaphors, like comparing therapy to a "helpful adventure" or "problem-solving game," to make it relatable. Gradually, the child gains insight into their own emotions and behaviors, recognizing that therapy is a space for exploration rather than judgment.

This understanding fosters a safe environment where children can address their concerns freely.

Overcoming Initial Resistance To Therapy

Resistance is common in Gestalt Play Therapy, especially with children who are new to therapy or hesitant about emotional expression.

To work through initial resistance, therapists often engage in non-directive play, allowing the child to take the lead. This approach reduces the perceived authority of the therapist and enables the child to explore the environment at their own pace, often resulting in a natural reduction of resistance.

Building a sense of autonomy is crucial to reducing resistance. Therapists can give children choices, such as which toys or activities to engage in, fostering a sense of control over the session. Through small decisions, children learn that therapy is a safe place where their preferences and voices matter. This empowerment helps ease resistance as the child sees the therapist as a partner rather than an authority.

When resistance persists, therapists might use metaphors or projective techniques. For instance, they might introduce a "reluctant" puppet who shares similar feelings, allowing the child to relate indirectly. By externalizing resistance through play, children feel validated and understood, making them more likely to open up. In this way, Gestalt Play Therapy creatively adapts to a child's resistance by embracing it as part of the therapeutic process.

Dealing With Intense Emotions And Outbursts

In Gestalt Play Therapy, children's intense emotions often surface through their play and interactions. The therapist's role is to create a supportive space where these emotions can be safely expressed without judgment. When a child experiences an emotional outburst, the therapist remains calm, modeling emotional regulation and allowing the child to experience the outburst fully. Validating the child's feelings during these moments helps them feel understood.

One technique to handle intense emotions is by using grounding activities, such as deep breathing or tactile play (e.g., squeezing clay or hugging a stuffed toy). These methods help the child re-center and manage their emotions more effectively. Therapists may also invite the child to "talk" through toys or draw their feelings, transforming emotions into something more manageable and less overwhelming.

To support children in learning self-regulation, therapists introduce concepts like naming feelings or creating "safe words" they can use when emotions feel too big. Over time, the child learns to recognize and label their emotions rather than becoming overwhelmed by them.

This process empowers children, equipping them with tools they can use outside of therapy to handle strong feelings constructively.

Managing Parent And Guardian Involvement

Parent and guardian involvement is integral to the success of Gestalt Play Therapy. Before sessions begin, therapists often meet with parents to understand their concerns and provide an overview of the therapy approach. This initial meeting sets expectations and explains that the focus will be on the child's emotional growth rather than solving specific problems immediately. Engaging parents in this way fosters trust and encourages their participation in the process. To ensure constructive involvement, therapists maintain open lines of communication with parents, updating them on progress and offering suggestions for supporting the child at home. Some therapists might teach parents basic play therapy techniques or mindfulness exercises that the child can practice outside sessions. This reinforces the therapeutic work and builds consistency between therapy and home environments.

However, boundaries must be respected to protect the child's therapeutic space. Therapists clearly outline what information will remain confidential and what will be shared. By establishing these guidelines, therapists help parents feel involved without crossing boundaries that might disrupt the child's sense of safety within the therapy space. This balanced approach supports both the child's autonomy and the family's engagement in the healing process.

Adapting Techniques For Different Ages

Gestalt Play Therapy requires flexibility in adapting techniques to the child's developmental stage. For younger children, therapists use sensory-based activities, such as finger painting or sensory bins, which engage their senses and encourage free expression. These activities allow children to explore feelings through tactile experiences, making it easier to express complex emotions in simple, age-appropriate ways. With school-aged children, therapists might incorporate more structured play elements, such as storytelling or role-playing games.

At this stage, children begin to develop more abstract thinking, making it possible for therapists to introduce characters and scenarios that reflect the child's inner conflicts. By using these indirect approaches, children feel less pressured and more willing to engage with their feelings and challenges.

Adolescents may need a combination of verbal processing and play. For this age group, therapists might integrate activities like journaling, art, or interactive games that allow for both self-reflection and creative expression. By recognizing the unique developmental needs of each age group, therapists can create tailored experiences that resonate more deeply with each child, fostering emotional growth and self-awareness in ways that feel relevant and accessible.

Handling Sensitive Topics And Trauma

Handling sensitive topics and trauma in Gestalt Play Therapy requires a gentle, trauma-informed approach. Therapists are careful to move at the child's pace, providing a steady, supportive presence.

When traumatic topics arise, therapists might use art or storytelling to create a safe distance, allowing children to process painful experiences without confrontation. This indirect approach helps children feel secure and allows emotions to surface gradually. To navigate these challenging areas, therapists use grounding techniques to help children stay present and centered.

Breathing exercises, grounding objects, or mindful observation activities can help children remain calm as they explore difficult memories or feelings. For example, a therapist might ask a child to focus on their breathing or to squeeze a comforting object when emotions intensify, anchoring them to the present moment. Therapists remain attuned to signs of distress and offer breaks when needed, respecting the child's emotional boundaries. Over time, these techniques help children build resilience and learn to process emotions connected to trauma safely. The ultimate goal is to empower children, providing them with coping tools that allow them to manage sensitive emotions both in and outside of the therapy room.

CHAPTER EIGHT

Detailed FAQs For Beginners

In Gestalt Play Therapy, the focus is on present-moment awareness and helping the child experience and processes their feelings through play rather than verbal dialogue. Frequently asked questions often include practical inquiries about how children's sessions are structured and how therapists address specific emotional needs.

A common question from beginners is how Gestalt Play Therapy supports the child's emotional growth compared to other therapeutic methods. Beginners often also ask how to handle disruptions during sessions, how often sessions should occur, and what kinds of tools are effective for facilitating play-based exercises.

Another common question relates to preparing a child for therapy. Parents and caregivers want to know how to introduce the idea of therapy and explain what will happen in sessions in ways the child will understand. It's generally helpful to let children know that the therapy session is a safe space where they can freely express themselves through toys, games, and other play activities. Parents are often guided to ensure that children feel safe and supported, encouraging them to view the session as an opportunity for self-exploration.

Lastly, many ask about the role of the therapist and how they facilitate emotional expression.

In Gestalt Play Therapy, the therapist is not just an observer but an active participant who interacts, guides, and sometimes models behaviors for the child. Therapists also help children identify their feelings, explore their inner world, and practice self-awareness. These FAQs provide a foundational understanding of what to expect, helping both parents and children feel more comfortable and ready for the journey.

How Does Gestalt Play Therapy Differ From Talk Therapy?

Gestalt Play Therapy distinguishes itself from traditional talk therapy by using play as a vehicle for self-expression, making it particularly effective for children who might struggle to articulate emotions verbally.

While talk therapy relies on direct conversation, Gestalt Play Therapy focuses on interactive activities such as role-playing, drawing, or storytelling. Through play, children express their emotions and thoughts without feeling pressured to verbalize them, which can make therapy feel more natural and less intimidating for young clients.

In Gestalt Play Therapy, the therapist's role is to observe and engage with the child's play to uncover underlying emotional themes. For example, a therapist might notice that a child consistently chooses a specific toy or reenacts certain scenarios, which can offer insights into their internal struggles or unresolved feelings. This active, observational approach allows the therapist to gently guide the child in processing these emotions, something less accessible in purely verbal interactions.

Another key difference is that Gestalt Play Therapy often utilizes activities that are physical or sensory-focused, which can be particularly grounding and help children better understand their emotions. By engaging the whole body and tapping into sensory experiences, Gestalt Play Therapy provides children with a holistic approach to self-exploration that can lead to deeper emotional understanding and resilience over time.

What Ages Benefit Most From Gestalt Play Therapy?

Gestalt Play Therapy is primarily beneficial for children ages 3 to 12, as this is a developmental stage when play is a primary means of learning and self-expression.

Younger children, particularly preschoolers, who may not have fully developed language skills, can find this type of therapy more accessible than talk-based approaches. Through play, they can express complex feelings and experiences they might not be able to verbalize.

For elementary school-aged children, Gestalt Play Therapy continues to offer significant benefits. At this age, children often experience a broadening social world and can face emotional challenges in relationships with peers, family, or at school. This therapeutic approach allows them to explore these dynamics in a safe, structured environment.

Through role-playing and other activities, children can rehearse different ways of handling social situations and work on building self-esteem.

Older children, around 10 to 12, can still benefit from Gestalt Play Therapy, particularly if they find it difficult to discuss their feelings directly. They might engage in more structured forms of play therapy that incorporate both verbal and play elements. These children are on the cusp of adolescence and may face emerging issues like self-identity, peer pressure, and independence. The therapist can adapt activities to encourage these children to connect playfully with their emotions while gradually introducing more reflective exercises.

How Can Parents Support Their Child's Therapy Journey?

Parental support is crucial in Gestalt Play Therapy, as parents provide the child with a sense of safety and validation outside of therapy. One of the most effective ways parents can support this process is by being open and communicative, setting a positive tone for therapy sessions. Before sessions, they might explain to the child that therapy is a fun, safe place where they can play and share anything they like without fear of judgment or punishment. This reassurance helps the child enter therapy with a positive mindset, which can lead to more productive sessions.

During the therapy process, parents can help reinforce the lessons learned in sessions by practicing at home. For instance, if a child is learning to express feelings of anger through drawing or storytelling in therapy, parents can create a similar activity at home to encourage the child to process their emotions. Additionally, respecting the child's privacy is essential; parents should avoid pressing them to disclose every detail of their sessions but instead offer an open ear if the child wishes to share.

After sessions, parents are encouraged to work collaboratively with the therapist to understand progress and any areas where they might need to adjust their approach. They can ask the therapist for specific guidance on how to support the child's growth, such as setting aside regular playtime or encouraging expressive activities. This partnership ensures that the therapeutic gains achieved in sessions extend into the child's daily life.

What Should A First Session Look Like?

A first session in Gestalt Play Therapy is typically designed to establish a sense of safety and rapport between the child and therapist. The therapist will start by creating a welcoming environment, often with a variety of toys, art supplies, and other materials that encourage exploration.

They may begin by allowing the child to freely choose an activity, observing how the child interacts with different toys, or responding to open-ended prompts. This unstructured play lets the therapist understand the child's interests and comfort level without pressuring them.

During this first meeting, the therapist's primary role is to build trust. They might engage in parallel play—playing alongside the child without direct interaction—until the child feels comfortable enough to include the therapist in their activities. The therapist uses this time to observe behaviors, emotional expressions, and any themes that naturally arise. For example, a child repeatedly arranging toys in a specific way may reveal their thoughts on structure, control, or security.

At the end of the first session, the therapist may provide some gentle feedback or validation to reinforce positive behaviors.

They also use this time to explain that future sessions will continue to be a safe space for exploring thoughts and feelings. This early emphasis on trust-building sets the stage for a productive therapeutic relationship and helps the child view the therapy space as their special place for self-expression.

What Tools And Resources Can Help In Therapy Sessions?

A variety of tools and resources can enhance the Gestalt Play Therapy experience by helping children explore their emotions and express themselves creatively. Common tools include sand trays, dollhouses, and puppet theaters, which allow children to enact different roles and scenarios that may reflect their feelings or experiences. Art supplies like crayons, markers, and clay provide a nonverbal way for children to convey complex emotions, and therapists often encourage children to create freely as part of their self-exploration.

Sensory tools, such as weighted blankets, stress balls, and textured items, can also play a role, especially for children who may experience anxiety or difficulty calming down. These resources help children feel grounded and present, enhancing their awareness of their physical sensations and feelings.

In addition to these tools, therapists may use guided imagery or storytelling exercises to stimulate children's imagination and explore different emotional states or situations in a gentle way.

Digital resources and apps designed for emotional regulation, such as mood trackers or meditation guides for kids, are becoming more common and can be integrated into therapy sessions.

These can help children engage with the therapeutic process in a way that feels modern and accessible. When used thoughtfully, these tools enrich therapy sessions and allow children to explore and express themselves in diverse and meaningful ways.

CHAPTER NINE

Tracking Progress And Evaluating Outcomes

In Gestalt play therapy, tracking progress is essential to ensure that therapy is beneficial to the child. This is often done through regular observations of the child's behaviors, emotional expressions, and engagement during sessions. Therapists use play activities as a way to gauge emotional development, self-awareness, and how the child interacts with their environment. For example, a child who becomes more willing to express feelings or take initiative in play may be showing signs of growth.

Evaluating outcomes involves looking for changes in how the child relates to others, how they manage emotions, and whether they can articulate their thoughts better over time. These observations are key to identifying whether the therapy is leading to meaningful improvements. Progress is often measured by comparing initial behaviors and emotional states with those exhibited after a few sessions. Both the child's feedback and input from caregivers play a role in understanding the progress made.

Therapists should also rely on creative tools like drawings, role-playing, and storytelling to help assess emotional changes. By observing recurring themes or shifts in how the child plays, therapists can recognize if the therapeutic goals are being met. Keeping open communication with the child's caregivers helps confirm whether progress made in sessions is also seen in everyday life.

Setting And Reviewing Goals With The Child

Setting clear, achievable goals with the child is an important first step in Gestalt play therapy. Goals should be aligned with the child's emotional needs, behavioral challenges, or relational difficulties.

At the beginning of therapy, the therapist and child, along with caregivers, collaboratively discuss what they hope to achieve. This could include goals like improving emotional regulation, building self-esteem, or reducing anxiety.

As therapy progresses, goals should be reviewed regularly to ensure they are still relevant and achievable. The therapist can use the child's play and creative activities to revisit these goals, encouraging the child to express whether they feel they are improving or facing new challenges. Open-ended questions, like "What would you like to change in your life?" help the child think about their progress.

Therapists also adapt goals as the child's needs evolve. If a child reaches one milestone, such as expressing their feelings more openly, new goals might be set to focus on deeper emotional understanding or improving social relationships. This flexible approach ensures that the child remains engaged in the therapeutic process and feels a sense of ownership over their progress.

Methods For Observing Emotional And Behavioral Changes

Observation is a critical part of Gestalt play therapy, where therapists closely monitor how the child interacts with their environment and expresses their feelings. Emotional changes may be seen in the way a child plays, with a shift from repetitive or avoidant behaviors to more explorative or creative play. For example, a child who was initially withdrawn might begin to express themselves more freely in role-playing or storytelling games.

Therapists use play materials like dolls, puppets, or art supplies to give the children opportunities to project their emotions. The therapist observes these sessions to see if the child's emotional expressions evolve. Sudden changes in behavior, such as moving from calm play to aggressive actions, can reveal underlying emotional struggles that need further exploration.

Additionally, therapists might look for signs of behavioral change outside of therapy by speaking with the child's caregivers. Improvements in school performance, better relationships with peers, or more consistent emotional regulation are indicators that the therapy is having a positive effect. Combining in-session observations with outside feedback helps therapists get a comprehensive view of the child's emotional and behavioral progress.

Keeping Session Notes And Reflective Journals

Maintaining session notes and reflective journals is essential for therapists practicing

Gestalt play therapy. After each session, the therapist should record key observations about the child's emotional state, the themes that emerged during play, and any significant behaviors. This allows the therapist to track progress over time and identify patterns in the child's development. These notes are also useful for planning future sessions and adjusting therapy techniques.

Reflective journaling allows therapists to process their emotional reactions and thoughts during therapy sessions. This self-reflection is important because it helps the therapist stay aware of their personal biases or emotional responses that could impact their work with the child. For example, if a therapist notices they are feeling frustrated or overly empathetic, they can adjust their approach to remain neutral and supportive.

Additionally, reviewing session notes and reflective journals regularly ensures that the therapist stays aligned with the therapeutic goals. By documenting what worked well in sessions and where challenges arose, therapists can fine-tune their methods to better meet the child's needs and ensure a consistent, effective therapeutic process.

Assessing Long-Term Benefits And Growth

Assessing long-term benefits in Gestalt play therapy involves looking beyond the immediate changes and observing how therapy impacts the child's overall emotional and psychological development.

Therapists measure this by noting whether the child's ability to self-regulate emotions, communicate effectively, and maintain healthy relationships improves over time. Positive shifts in self-awareness and emotional resilience are signs of long-term growth.

To gauge long-term success, therapists also consider how the child handles real-life situations outside of therapy. Caregiver feedback on how the child responds to stress, manages conflicts, or expresses emotions in day-to-day life is crucial for understanding the lasting impact of therapy.

A child who learns to express frustration through words instead of acting out, for instance, is showing evidence of long-term benefit.

Periodic evaluations over several months or years can help determine if the therapy has created a solid foundation for the child's ongoing emotional health. Long-term growth can also be seen in the child's increased ability to adapt to new situations or challenges with greater confidence and emotional stability.

Adjusting Therapy Approaches Based On Progress

As the child progresses in Gestalt play therapy, it is essential for the therapist to adjust their approach to match the evolving needs of the child.

In the beginning, therapy may focus on building trust and encouraging emotional expression through simple play. As the child becomes more comfortable, the therapist can introduce more complex activities that challenge the child to explore deeper emotions or difficult experiences.

Therapy adjustments might also involve shifting the focus from emotional exploration to skill-building, such as teaching coping strategies or enhancing social skills. If a child has made significant progress in one area, such as reducing anxiety, the therapist may begin to work on other challenges like improving communication or self-esteem.

Therapists should remain flexible and responsive, using regular check-ins with both the child and their caregivers to determine if the therapy is meeting the child's current needs. By continually adapting techniques and goals, the therapist ensures that the therapy remains relevant and beneficial throughout the child's developmental journey.

Conclusion

The conclusion of a "Complete Guide to Gestalt Play Therapy" encapsulates the essence and transformative potential of Gestalt play therapy, emphasizing its unique, holistic approach to supporting children's emotional and psychological development. This therapeutic model centers around the here-and-now experience, promoting awareness and self-acceptance in children by engaging them in creative and expressive play.

By integrating foundational Gestalt principles such as awareness, contact, and the use of present experiences, Gestalt play therapy allows children to access their emotions, process experiences, and develop healthier ways of relating to themselves and others.

A key takeaway is the flexibility and adaptability of Gestalt play therapy to meet the varied needs of each child, respecting their developmental stage and individuality.

The approach emphasizes the therapist's attunement to the child, building a therapeutic alliance that is compassionate, authentic, and empowering. Through techniques like role-playing, storytelling, art, and movement, children are given tools to explore their feelings, work through conflicts, and build resilience. The therapist's role as an empathetic and nonjudgmental presence fosters a safe space, encouraging children to explore and make sense of complex emotions and experiences at their own pace.

In summary, the conclusion of this guide underlines that Gestalt play therapy is an effective method for fostering self-discovery and healing in children. It encourages therapists to maintain a grounded understanding of Gestalt principles while applying creative techniques tailored to each child's needs.

This therapy emphasizes growth and self-support, aiming to empower children by enhancing their awareness, autonomy, and capacity for meaningful connections. By integrating Gestalt play therapy into clinical practice, therapists can provide impactful support, helping children build healthier emotional lives and relationships.

Ultimately, the guide reiterates the significance of Gestalt play therapy as a powerful modality for fostering resilience and authentic self-expression in young clients.

THE END

www.ingramcontent.com/pod-product-compliance
Lightning Source LLC
Chambersburg PA
CBHW061049250726
48653CB00001B/319